INSIDE
OF
ME

Struggles of the Heart and Mind

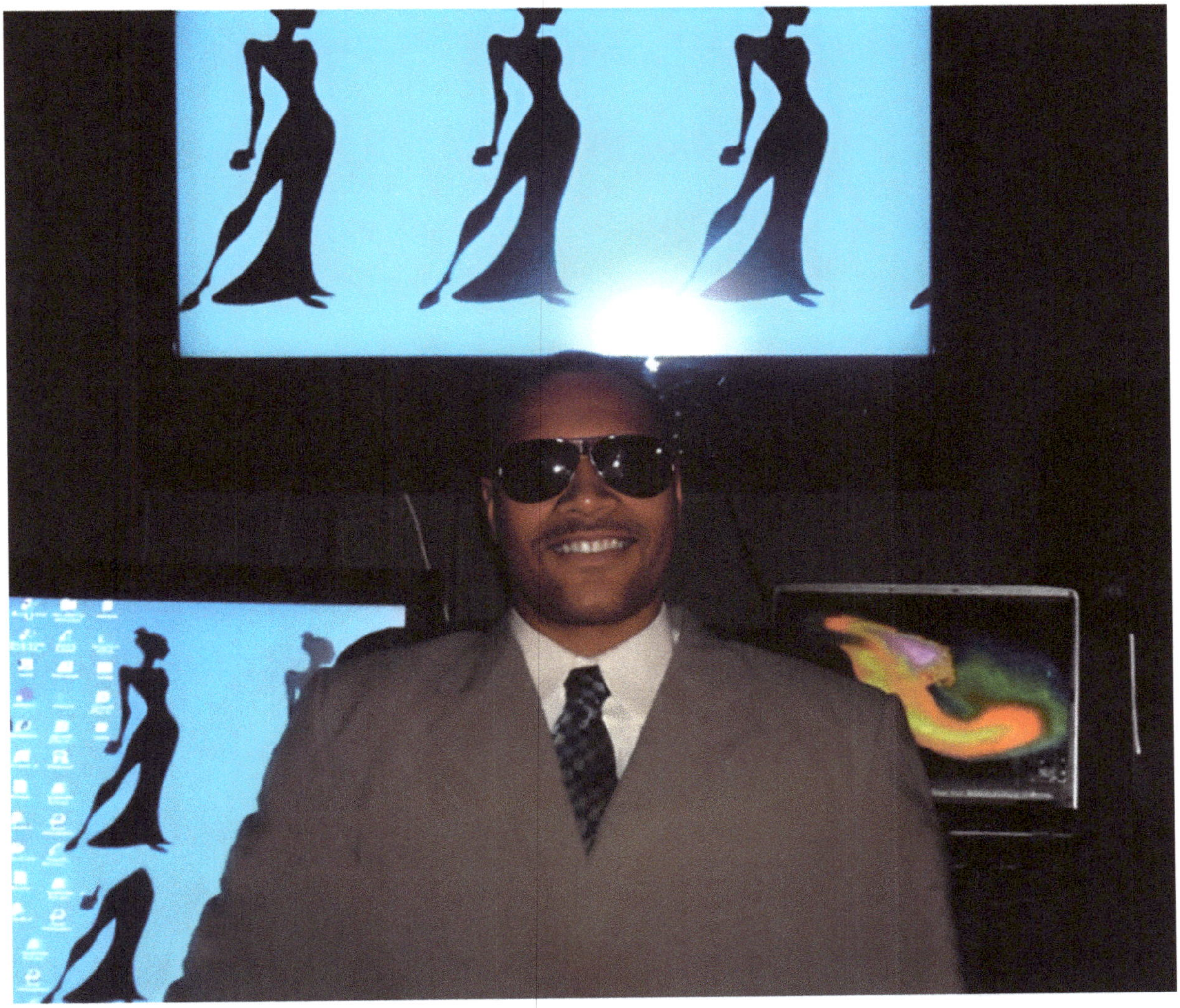

Inside of Me
Copyright © 2023 by Antony J. Gregory

ISBN
978-1-961601-07-9 (Paperback)
978-1-961601-08-6 (eBook)
978-1-961601-06-2 (Hardcover)

Table of Contents

The Inside of Me

All through my life
I've wondered how people
Thought of my outside
Along with my outside
There came my inside
I then took a glance at my inside
What I saw was heartbreak
Mental Struggles
That I just could not shake
Having the need to refigure me
Also searching to find who I were
Not too much living the standards of others
But doing the right thing
On a quest to better myself
Living life to survive
To hold on to close friends
To be strong
Where I reside
Only to keep it truthful
One hundred percent of the time
Even if having to place aside my pride

By: Antony J. Gregory

Forgot About Yesterday

Forgot about yesterday
Started to think about tomorrow
What does my future hold
Where do I belong
Where is my place in society
Once thought ten years ahead

Now is ten years ago
Dreaming of success
While continuously growing old
Later counting my blessings
Could I really do it
Could I ever make it
Out of my neighborhood
And actually become successful
Making someone out of me
Started to think some more
Finally came to the conclusion
Sometimes what seem
too difficult in life

Only take the simplest answer
To solve them so easy

By: Antony J. Gregory

Give You the World

If you could pick one place
What place would that be
Would it be on a cruise
Taking a vacation to Paris
Could it be right here next to me
If you could have one wish
Of what would that wish consist

Would it be a new car
Could it be new clothes
Perhaps a wish for
eternal life together
Pertaining of only
you and me
All I want to do is
give you the world
Allow me to your whole
world in my hands
Looking back at
our history
When it's finally over

Being able to say I was that man
Who've kept his promise
To never let you go
And do everything necessary
To be your man
That's my plan
To give you the world

By: Antony J. Gregory

Inspirational

They call me a hero
Because of the fact that I am inspirational
Saving the lost
The confused
The Weak
Persuasive words I speak
Full of thought

Full of knowledge
Full of love
Where could they run
For the do not know the way
Neither do they know the place
Inspirational is my name
But I can not inspire myself
Empty I am
All by myself

By: Antony J. Gregory

A Peace of Mind

Where can I find peace of mind
Distancing myself away from the things of
this world
Where can I find a piece of time
For it is all used up

Where can I find peace of mind
My mind has left its soul
Searching for its heart
Where has it gone
Peace of Mind
If you hear me
Please come my way
Please come to me soon
As soon as you can
Can you today
Finally a peace of mind

By: Antony J. Gregory

Looking Back to Memory Lane

I sit here to reminisce
Taking a look back to memory lane
A brief look in my past
Only to wonder
Did I correct every mistake

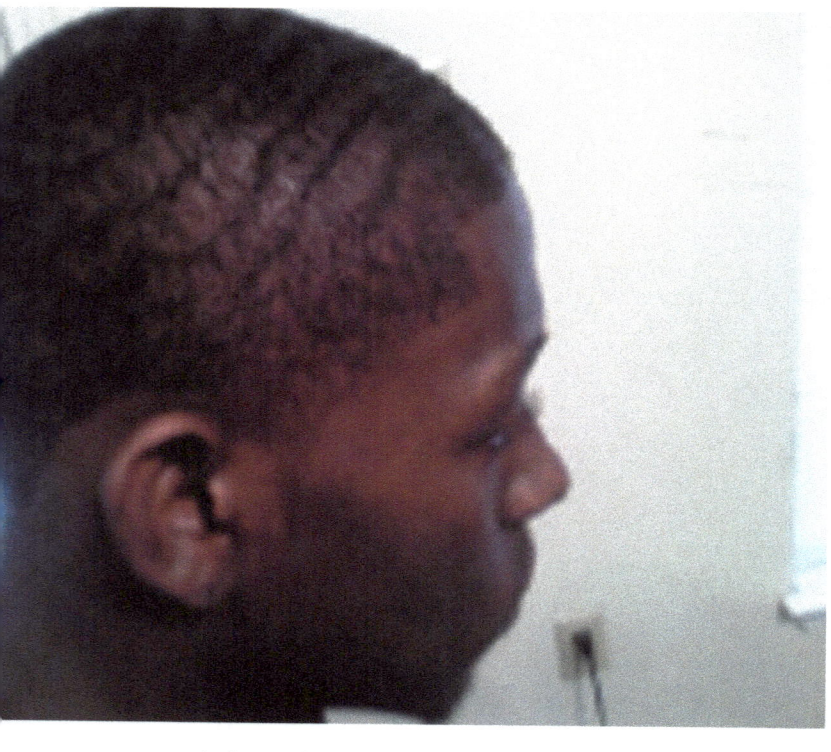

Have I learned the lessons
From which I anticipated
a concept
I sit here to reminisce
Still in memory lane
Still shocked to know
That time flies by so fast
Still questioning myself
Self
Will you make those
same mistakes
Have you learned to avoid them
Are those mistakes preventable
Still I wonder

Therefore
I am back to memory lane

By: Antony J. Gregory

Just a Thought

I sit here thinking
What is the definition of love
What qualities in a woman
Am I looking for
I guess it is just a thought

I sit here asking
Is love on this earth
Or is love found in heaven
Don't I feel like I'm in heaven
When I am in love
I guess I am thinking too much
Maybe I am thinking too little
Just a thought

By: Antony J. Gregory

Climbing These Mountains

Climbing these mountains
Doing it for far too long
One after another
Striving towards perfection

Still climbing these mountains
Falling a couple of times
Having to catch myself
Having to pull myself back up
Never falling completely
Because of one of the greatest fears
Failure
Climbing these mountains
The mind growing strong
Due to the journey ahead of me
Seeming so long
While climbing these mountains

By: Antony J. Gregory

Almost There

Almost there
Almost to the finish line
I can almost taste it
Feel it
Hear it

Smell it
There goes success
Almost there
The time seeming to move
slower by the minute
Wanting success right now
With it so close
It doesn't seem fair
Almost there
How am I able to hasten the time
Wish I were allowed a remote
Only to press fast forward
Never rewind
Almost there
Keeping that in mind

By: Antony J. Gregory

Who Am I?

Who am I
Still in chains and shackles
Bounded by itself
There by itself
Standing alone in the world
Who am I
Confined to the room

Only walls
Corner to corner
No doors
Who am I
Words cannot describe its mind
Too much going on in its head
Holding too many thoughts
Possessing a small amount of time
Who am I
Do I have a name
Could I be make-believe
Who am I
I guess I am me

By: Antony J. Gregory

The People

What would the world be without the people
Living day after day
Awaiting a better day
Searching for riches and fame
Undergoing tough times and pain

Some strain
To become the best that they can be
The people
Sharing the same goals
With no ambitions to collaborate
To make a plan
Everyone for self
Man for man
The people

By: Antony J. Gregory

Sweet like Candy

Your love and touch
Are both sweet like candy
From the first time we've met
Until our last good-bye
To explain what we are
Is unexplainable
Untamable the feelings that we have residing inside
Because of receiving a kiss from your lips
Caused me to want more and more
Crying out to see you again

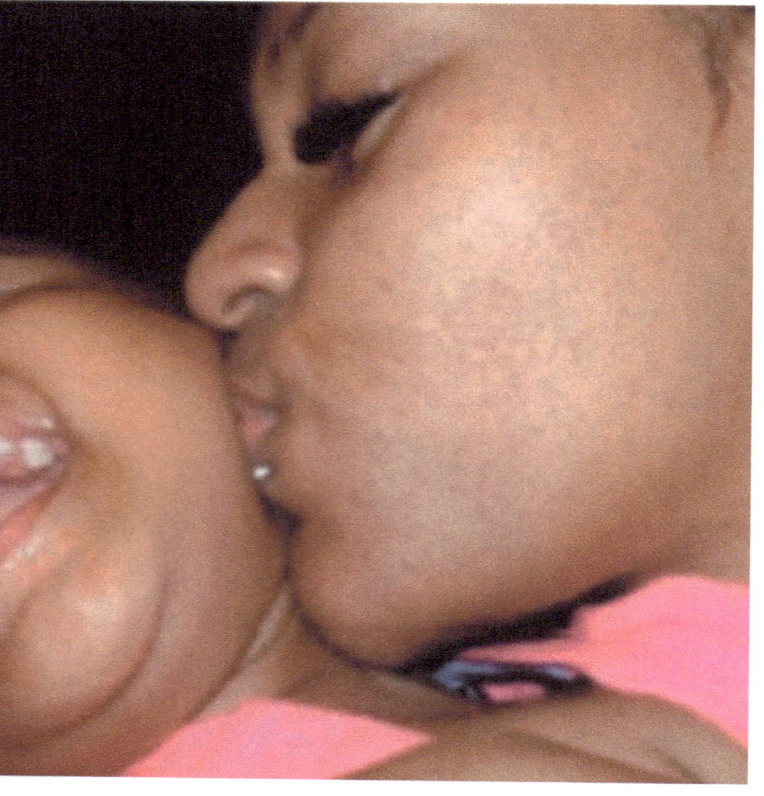

But your reply
"Silence is the key"
Therefore
No words were said
The boundaries of my heart led
To a place similar to
honeycomb and gold
The promise land

By: Antony J. Gregory

Missing You

Time is still ticking
Day is ending and night is approaching
The same routine the day after
Thinking about me and you
How we used to be

How we used to play
Smiling at one another
Every time we see one another's face
Behind closed doors
Only love we made
No one there but us
I'm missing you
Still trying to figure you out though
You are yet a mystery
But what can I say
I'm still awaiting your return
I'm missing you

By: Antony J. Gregory

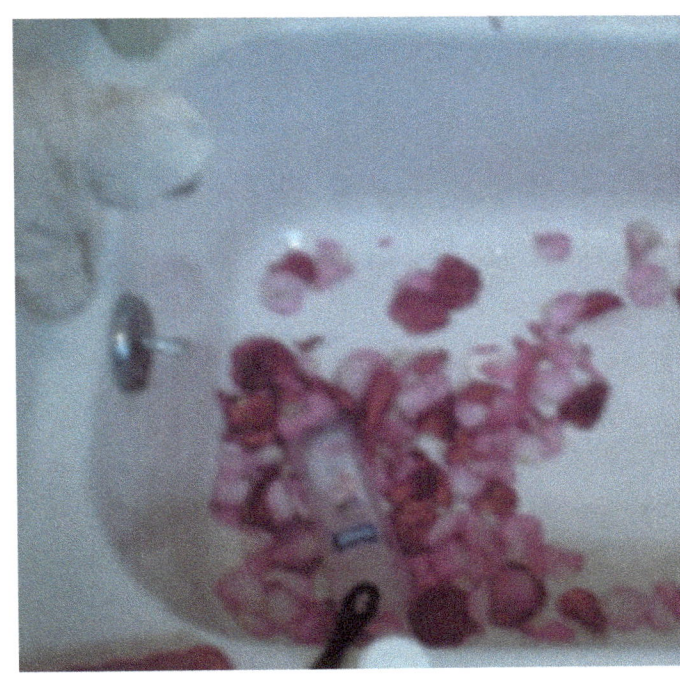

In the Clouds

In the clouds
Hidden from misery
Disaster
Traumatized events
Everything's so clouded
Been gone for some time
Where had I went
Where had I been
Where was I sent
Still I wonder
How could I fly
With no wings attached
So why would I try
Still I ponder
I feel nothing but wind

So cold in the air
So cold in my sins
Is this where I go
When I do my wrongs
Or is this where I go
When I do right
Maybe I've reached the light
Maybe I haven't
I realize what this is
A weird dream I was having

By: Antony J. Gregory

Never Enough

When I cook
Clean
Rub your feet
Dream
Why is it never enough
When I dress clean

To place rose peddles at your feet
Love you
Why are you never satisfied
Why is it never enough
Mean words are said
An apology isn't heard of
Although you are so wrong
And have the nerve to say
Why aren't you home
My home is out of this atmosphere
Where many show me love
So again I ask

Why is it never enough
I guess I only got me
The only person I must

By: Antony J. Gregory

A Matter of Time

It is a matter of time
Until you see the man which I've become
The one who seemed to be always loosing
But now has risen
And now has won
It is a matter of time
Was never able to be critiqued

Now able to
Only constructively
On a mission to better me
Only to tell others
Not just better me
Instead better we
We as a community
We as a people
We as a human race
Being able to do the things we love to do
To be able to do the things we wish we could
To take time out to think
About what we could

What we should
Yet still could
It is only a matter of time

By: Antony J. Gregory

The One for Me

Could it be
That you of all people be
The one for me
To explain she
Would first have to explain he
The one for me
Intelligent
Funny
Outgoing
Goal Oriented
The one for me
Lovable
In spite of flaws

To lose that love
Would be a loss
Could it be
You
The one for me

By: Antony J. Gregory

Objective Complete

Everyday
Every minute
Every second
Dreaming of success
Even then
Will my objective be complete
Good job

Good Effort
As long as I knew
I've put forth as much effort as possible
Never giving up
Survival of the fittest
Know that
I can only save myself
I was sent on the life long journey
All by myself
My objective
Is almost done
Not yet completed
Until my life shows
Objective complete

By: Antony J. Gregory

Walking a Thin Rope

Walking a thin rope
Just can not seem to walk straight
Too many thoughts running through my mind
What baggage will I leave
What will I take
What do I need
What is it that I don't
What goals in this life will I accomplish
What are the goals in which I won't

When will I make it
Off this thin rope I walk
Don't want to fall off
But it's hard to stay on top
Thoughts of taking a break
Just a little time off
But if I do that
When will I get through
So I just keep walking
To accomplish being a winner
With no intentions to lose

By: Antony J. Gregory

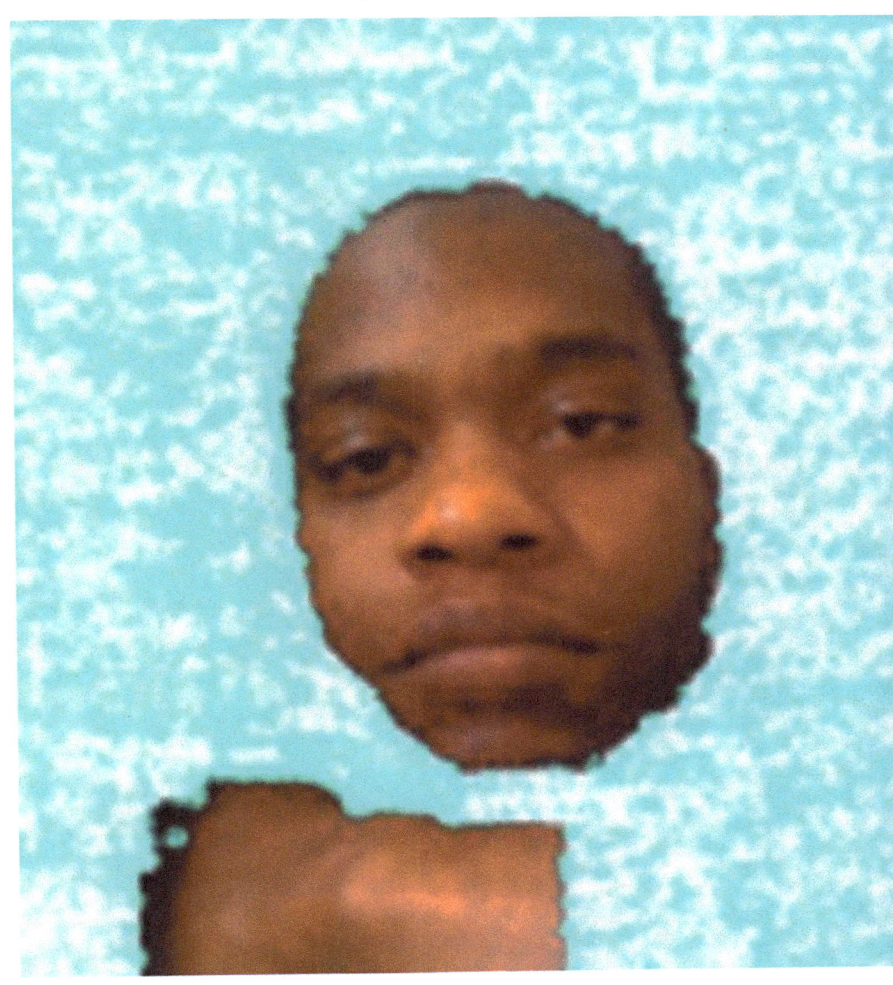

A Never Ending

Sunshine
Be patient
A never ending sunshine
A never ending sunshine
Life is feeling great
Where the possibilities are limitless
From when waking to brush my teeth
Where the wind blows in your favor
Until the time for my nights' break
And you bypass those hypocrites
A never ending sunshine
Sitting back to implement
Everything seems unreal
A never ending sunshine
I feel lovely out here
Please stay longer

Just sitting back to chill
My circadian clock is waking me up
A never ending sunshine,
Most definitely making me stronger
Will the sunshine ever stop
Not for a minute I hope
Feeling like I am the man on top
Similar to the pope
Giving other people hope
By the people seeing my sunshine
Maybe I will lead a nation
Since the sun is shining right now
I think I can wait

By: Antony J. Gregory

Who Has the Answers

Who has the answers
You know I have asked around
Why does life have ups
Why does life have downs
If you're rich
Are you happy
If you're poor
Are you sad
Or are you mad
Which one is it
Money is not everything
That is what many people say
Still it buys the car you drive
The food you eat
You are able to have fun
Any given time
Any given day
So if it buys all of this
Why can't we buy love
Who has the answers
Please let me know
I've been searching you know
And still
My questions don't go
They grow

By: Antony J. Gregory

A Window to Set

You Free

People who are just as determined as I am

Trapped in this dark place

To make it out

Four walls

Of a place of four walls

A toilet

A dirty toilet

A bed

A hard bed

Toilet so dirty

Which if I had stay

Nobody there but me

Eventually would have had

Then I saw a window

A hardhead

That I saw could set me free

Having little or no value

I then begin to go to the window

Similar to a worthless piece of trash

Everyone there began to start pulling me back

Everyone would see through me

They said don't go

As if I were a piece of glass

Just stay with us

So now I am here

Just relax

Trying to stay here
I could not
Where everyone counts
Although there I thought to have many friends
But if I don't make it
Friends that I would hurt me
If I cannot do it
So I said no
What is my life about
And that I have other plans
With other friends
Who I know won't hurt me
Those who are on the same page as me

By: Antony J. Gregory

Please Come Back

I don't know why I left
Please come back
Maybe since things happen for a reason
Please don't leave this way

Was it a test
I know I made a mistake
I know it was stress
I know I stayed away
Dealing with the aftermath
As well as played the games I played
Please come back
Well I am sorry
I just don't know what to do
Is enough to say
Do me this favor
Or is that too small
And I promise

Am I too late
To never again hurt you
Have you found someone
You are my queen
Who can make you feel the way that I do
And I need you by my side
Are they making you feel butterfl ies
Myself a king
Making you groove
With so much pride

Please come back
Please come back
I'm begging on my knees
If you do
Begging for your forgiveness
I will never let you go
I am begging you
I promise to take care of your every need
Please
I also promise to hold you close
Please come back
To cherish every minute that we spend
together
Like it were my last
And to give you the world
Whatever it is that you may ask
Just please come back
Don't leave me this way
You were a blessing sent from God
So to God I pray
That you return
Please come back

By: Antony J. Gregory

That One Girl

That one girl
That you never wanted to lose
To your pride you lost
Now soft
Because things turned upside down
That one girl you left
For the girl you felt
Would and could be that one
Was not

Now you're alone
That one girl
The one whom once loved you
Is still there
Yet she's gone
She let you decide
Therefore
You left on your own
Going where you wanted to be
Whether in the wilderness
Or at home
What will it be

That one girl said
Sincerely
Also hurt
Wondering would you make the right choice
She has moved on
Now evaluating everything

You sit there
Looking for her voice
Where did she go
What have I done
She was right for me
She was the one

By: Antony J. Gregory

Looking in the Mirror

Entering adulthood
As I look in the mirror,
Confused of which direction to go
In it is what I see of myself
Not knowing which way to turn
My past
Not knowing will I make it through the
My present
struggles of life
My future
Or when I make it to the point in life to teach
My health
my children
My wealth
When it is their turn to learn
As I look into the mirror
It's my turn
I think to myself

My parents have warned me before
What can I do
Now I am here
To make me better
Looking in the mirror
I think inside the box
Wondering what to do next
Then my mind starts to wonder
I guess I will find out

What do I need to do
In due time
To make it over the hill yonder
I guess
Beyond my imagination
Me looking towards the future
And not right now
Is where my time went
Me in the mirror
What do I see about myself
A lost man

By: Antony J. Gregory

Just the Way it is

Just thinking to myself
Why aren't my questions ever answered
Why am I always deep into thought
Does being an important figure mean being
pampered
Or is the boat you just bought
Just the way it is

Either riches and fame
Or struggle with kids
Working hard to survive and provide
But living to die
Can we honestly say happiness is found either way
Or continue living a lie
Just the way it is

By: Antony J. Gregory

In It Confused

Alone in this house,
Thinking of you day after day
Will you ever return
From this crazy world
Will you return to stay

In it confused
Don't know if you care like I do
If you want my heart like I do
I asked you to express yourself
To tell me how you felt inside
In it confused
Tell me that we are not living a lie
That I am the one you think about at night
Am I the one for the rest of your life

I really need to know
If not please go
Far way
Never to see me again
In it confused

By: Antony J. Gregory

Close to my Heart

I get close to you
Kissing your lips softly
Holding your body tight
Never wanting to let go
You're getting close to my heart

Sometimes thinking of letting you go
My heart keeps saying no
It tells me to stop
As well as controlling my actions
Revealing to me
How to touch your body
Also how to heal your heart
That it I may sooth
If I ever lost your love
Or what feels like it
Infatuation
Where would I be now
Eager to find love
My heart is slowly dying
Because of you missing
I'm trying to patch my heart together
Each piece that falls off of it
Glitters and shimmers onto the ground
Never to see that spark again
Not even to hear a sound

By: Antony J. Gregory

The Heart You Tore Apart

Woman
You really broke my heart
Got a good guy like me
Sitting alone in the dark
I wish we would've worked out
But you left me though
You left me broke
Right when winter was approaching
Left me in the cold
With possibility of snow

Where cold I go
What could I do
I never wanted to hurt you
Because of the love that I have for you
I gave you all I had
Placed you before me
Until you got rude also childish
You broke my heart
What more can I say
I still love you
From the bottom of my heart
The heart that you tore apart

By: Antony J. Gregory

Where Had I

Gone Wrong
Still you couldn't catch on
I gave you all I had
To the hints
Still you were not satisfied
Along with late night conversations
Where had I gone wrong

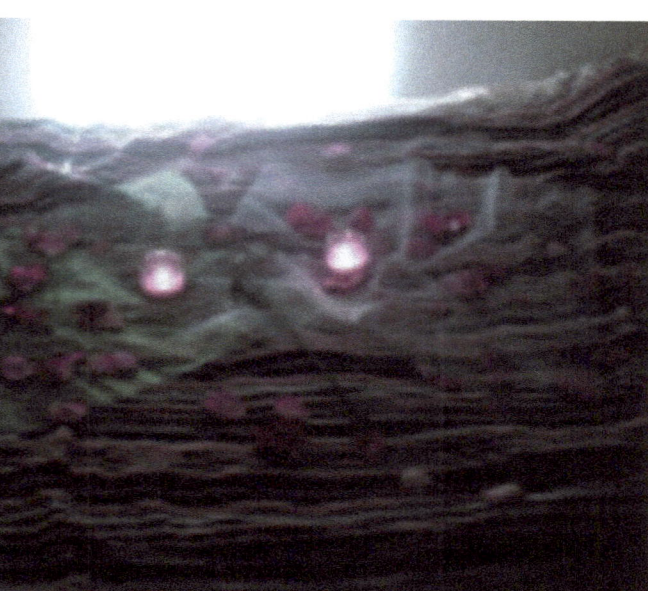

Telling you that I wanted a family with you
I gave you space
I figure you are not ready for a happy home
When you needed it
Therefore we can't be together
Just to let you breathe
I'd rather be alone
Yet we both felt overcrowded
Just to heal me
In love
To be able to deal with the reality of
The things people will do for love

the matter
Not knowing whether you have found
That once we were in love
that one
No longer in love anymore
Still willing to go that extra mile
A page in history written
Just to make things work

Could we go back into time

Still waiting for a change

For just more time

Still nothing seems to be changing at all

So I sit here asking myself

Emotions floating everywhere

Where had I gone wrong

Heart shattered

Because of the time wasted

Giving you chance after chance

Time and time again

By: Antony J. Gregory

I Would Rather Say

Good Morning
It feels as if I'm lost
I would rather say good morning
I then begin to question myself
Rather than saying good bye
Where have my life gone
Being able to be around
Your smile brightens my day

After you have come from a long day at work
It feels as though I am in heaven
Asking how your day went
Like I have the whole in my hands
I would like to be involved
When holding you close
In every aspect of your life
I feel as if I were home
You are just so beautiful
Never let me go
From your head to your toe
Although we must say good-bye
When you're sassy

You will continue to live in my heart
Mad or happy
Me still saying
I would rather say good morning
I would rather say good morning
After we have had a long night

Rather arguing
Or making sweet love
I would say good night to say good morning
One day without you
My day is all wrong

By: Antony J. Gregory

Not sincere

You have made the same mistake
Time and time again
Telling me that you apologize
Even though you were not sincere
Now that we are separated
I have replaced you
And have found someone new
You cannot seem to accept the fact

To see me away from you
The truth of the matter being
That I no longer love you
You still love me
You still care
You say you want me back
But I don't know if I can
Take you back
Because when we were together
You were not sincere.

By: Antony J. Gregory

Knowing Not

How can we hang out
When I'm knowing that we wont
How can I say I love you
Knowing deep in my heart that I don't
How can I let you know where we are going
Knowing that I can't
Or can I
How can I explain
Why keep dragging your heart

I know why
While you know not
You are wondering in the dark
While I am walking in the light
Still you wonder
Will he answer me
Will he take me out
He just might
He may not

By: Antony J. Gregory

Living Sacrifice

Always giving,
Going through life,
Sacrificing throughout it
Still bonded to pay bills
No time for any excitement
Can I have a break
Any down time I will take
I need five minutes

Please
Why the rush
You can not wait
What price is able to solve it
Do I sacrifice my whole life
I can not believe it
Why do you want money
Why need it
Beat it
I don't see it.

By: Antony J. Gregory

The Black Man

The black man
Full of pride
Full of power
Hardworking
Day by day and every hour
Making time for his marriage
Also making time for his mistress
Possessing so much ego
Because of everything he has accomplished
Visualizing everything he wishes
Striving to make him the best that he could
possibly be
The best that a black man can
Sometimes proud to say
I am a black man
Times get hard
Still the black man holds on strong
When everyone doubts he will succeed
He still rolls on
Life still goes on
Until that black man finds redemption
Searching to find himself
The black man walks angry
Causing him to blind himself
The one thing the black man is missing
Never mind others
Mind himself

By: Antony J. Gregory

The Black Woman

She is strong mentally
Always thinking a lot and feels
Of everything that goes on
In the past
The present
And will
Yet still
Keeps her head held high
Through the turmoil
Within her surroundings

And the boys she encounters
throughout her life
Searching for that man
That one man
Who will come and rock her world
Only this will happen for the black woman
And not that black girl
Living in a world
Full of business
Pleasure and lust
Because of all encounters with liars
Cheaters
Backstabbers
Who can she trust
Love
She follows her heart
Where she has ended up later

Happy

Is far from which she has begun

Her journey

Long yet she learns

To whom she will go

To whom she can turn

By: Antony J. Gregory

Why Still Hold On

Why am I still holding on
Why haven't I let you go
Why to whatever you want I can always say yes
And saying to you goodbye I can always say no
Maybe I know weather you are truly in love with me
Or if it is infatuation
Because of when going out to eat
I always know how to make you laugh
Our conversation consisting of
All our good times
Never worrying about the bad
Even when you make me mad
You know how to make that up
When I am away do you get any sleep
Or do you wake back up

Wishing I were there
to hold you close
Why am I still holding on
Maybe I realize I need you most

By: Antony J. Gregory

Until the End

Until the end of the world
You will have me on you side
Until the end of my life
Struggling to make a difference
Even when making a difference
Seems not to be effective
Until to my last breathe
Can I hold your hand
When I feel there is not a reason to live
Nor a reason to give

All that I have being trying
My soul is leaving my body
Feeling though as I am flying
Or am I floating
I am dying
Until the end

By: Antony J. Gregory

I wonder

I wonder
To myself why lie
What is the point of life
When in fact the truth hurts
Walking back and forth
Are we born to pass time
Pondering

I am lost and can not seem to find myself
Too much into thought
I see the truth of it all
With my mind wandering
So I don't blind myself
Am I confused
Was I born to make friends
Here stuck at a crossroad
Or should I mind myself
Should I give up now
Am I here to compete with others
Because if and when I make it to the top
And after there is no one left to compete with
Where do I go

Time myself
What is the point of being the riches
man alive
What profits a man to gain the whole world

and lose his soul

Besides

I can't take any of my possessions with me

when I die

So why even try

By: Antony J. Gregory

Leave Me Alone

With you I am going insane
Leave Me Alone
So now I am done
I no longer have anything to say
I no longer have anything to say
We have gone down this road before
How could you do this to me
Once Again
How could you have played the games

I do not see myself headed that way
you've played
I need time to think
When you told me that you loved me
Are you and I meant to be
How can I believe your words
There is no "I" in team
Words coming from your mouth
There in only "I" in me
Feel as though I am standing
So how is there an "I" in we
In a place full of mist
Maybe this is not worth it

I can't see anything
Nothings seems to change
My view is all a blur
You do the same things
Since you can't figure me out

I have asked you not to
Neither can I you
Now that we are separated
Leave me alone
Am I responsible of the blame
Again I say
To me
Leave me alone for good
To you this is just fun and games
Please leave me alone

By: Antony J. Gregory

Picture this

Picture this
Today belongs to you
Somehow I've managed to get rich
Picture this
Spend as much as you can
If I was the poorest man alive
Spend as much as you wish
Would you still love me
As long as your love stays strong

Would you still hold me close
And when you leave this world of ours
Would you let me stay at your house
I am the one whom you come home
Would you love me most
Picture this
If I could not provide the better things in life
We can travel the world
And we couldn't go to see a beach
With me all to yourself
What if I aim high in life
Just you and I alone
But my goals
And no one else
Were too high to reach
Picture this
Would you love me
The only way to your goals

Or could you not picture that

Is to imagine it

Would we be intimate

Is to picture it

Or would you imply

We are walking on a beach

That I stink too bad

Viewing the sunset

That you would not touch me

Also feeling the cool breeze

Thinking I were insane

Blowing through your hair

To try to capture your beauty

The sand soft

Picture this

Below our feet

We are the only ones left alive

Seeing that your body being beautiful

In the world and everyone else died

I feel as though my composure I can not

Would you be able to love me

maintain

Even if you tried

I have to take a look

Or would you let me die

You seem to be the most beautiful thing

Later you die

I've seen

Therefore the world dies

In a very long time

Picture that

The water drops from the sea
Glistening falling from your body
The tan you have just acquired
Looking as though you are an angel
We go to the beach house
Relaxing for a minute
Later doing whatever you like

By: Antony J. Gregory

Still in love

That leads us to feel this way
When you are still in love
Still in your mind
You keep holding on
Sitting alone visualizing
Never letting go

IS this the person whom
I would like to
Similar to holding on
to your last breath
grow old
Knowing that it is almost out
Still shocked to find that
you still don't know
When you are still in love
Knowing that for
the time being
There is that one person
You feel as though
you are in love

That you just can not seem to shake from
That person you are thinking of
your mind
The one you are continuously trying to shake
That is the one
Even if you are continuously going places
You are always thinking of all the time

You are thinking of them
You are wondering what they are up to
When you work
Later asking to yourself
While you are eating
Are they thinking of me
When you wake
As much I am thinking of them
I think I know how to relax
Are they reminiscing
Eat ice cream and eat cake
Are they going back into time
Still love is on my mind
Viewing all the good time spent together
Why
You start to question again
You ask yourself that love is on my mind
How do I stay stuck on someone
Maybe you are still in love
It is a difficult answer to explain
Easiest to say there are forces
Beyond our control

By: Antony J. Gregory

Seeing You Once More

Seeing you once more
After seeing you once more
I made you smile
Your smile relieve all the pain I had
You made me too
built up inside

The reason why
The hurt
I feel as though I cannot stop loving you
The suffering
Seeing you once more
All the tears I've cried
Is all that I needed to do
All that was gone
Finding that you still care
Everything immediately was placed to
After seeing me once more
the side
And me still caring about you
You were the main topic
I had not seen you in so long
By: Antony J. Gregory

And since I had the privilege
I cherished it
A reminder of
How the kiss from your lips felt
As well as being in your presence
How've you smelled
Caused me to understand
Why you I should've not left

Just Hoping

Should I run
Walking along side one another
Should I stay
Holding on to one anothers hand
Concerned of the strength of our emotions

Stealing kisses on the slide
Myself feeling as though I should push
What more can I ask for
them away
Just hoping
Just hoping
Maybe just wishing
This may be where my
true love may reside
Hopefully things will stay the same
This risk I am willing to take
All throughout this love thing
To find out if this is real
Through our ups and downs
Or just one big lie
Overcoming the happy moments and
Who knows for sure

the pouts
I sigh while wondering
Keeping our love strong
Where everything may end
Is what our love is about

Is this the end
With our feelings so strong
Or is this where I begin
Everything feeling like magic
While I am waiting
Your lips and body so soft
All I can do is hope
Will things stay the same
Just hoping
Maybe just thinking
How could this get any better

By: Antony J. Gregory

What Can I Do

I used to feel special
What can I do
I just felt this the other day
When everything has been done

Today I am lonely
What can I say
In a room all to myself
When there is nothing left to say
My mind is too crammed
How should I feel
To develop feelings for someone else
When I felt so much that I can no longer
Again I ask
feel a thing
What can I do
Having my emotions so discombobulated
When everything has been done
It has started to drive me insane
What can I say
I can not stress

How am I to carry on
With you my stress has finally run out
I have tried everything
Run out so much
I have said that can be said
That I have lost sense
I hold told you I love you

Of the meaning of stress
Until my face have turned blue now red
With my feelings crushed
So what do I do
Still my heart broken
When I have done all that could be done
I can feel it in my chest
I run
Why
I ask to myself
Why must I feel this way

By: Antony J. Gregory

Headed for the Stars

Headed for the stars
So get out of my way
Nothing is a game anymore
No time to joke
No time to play

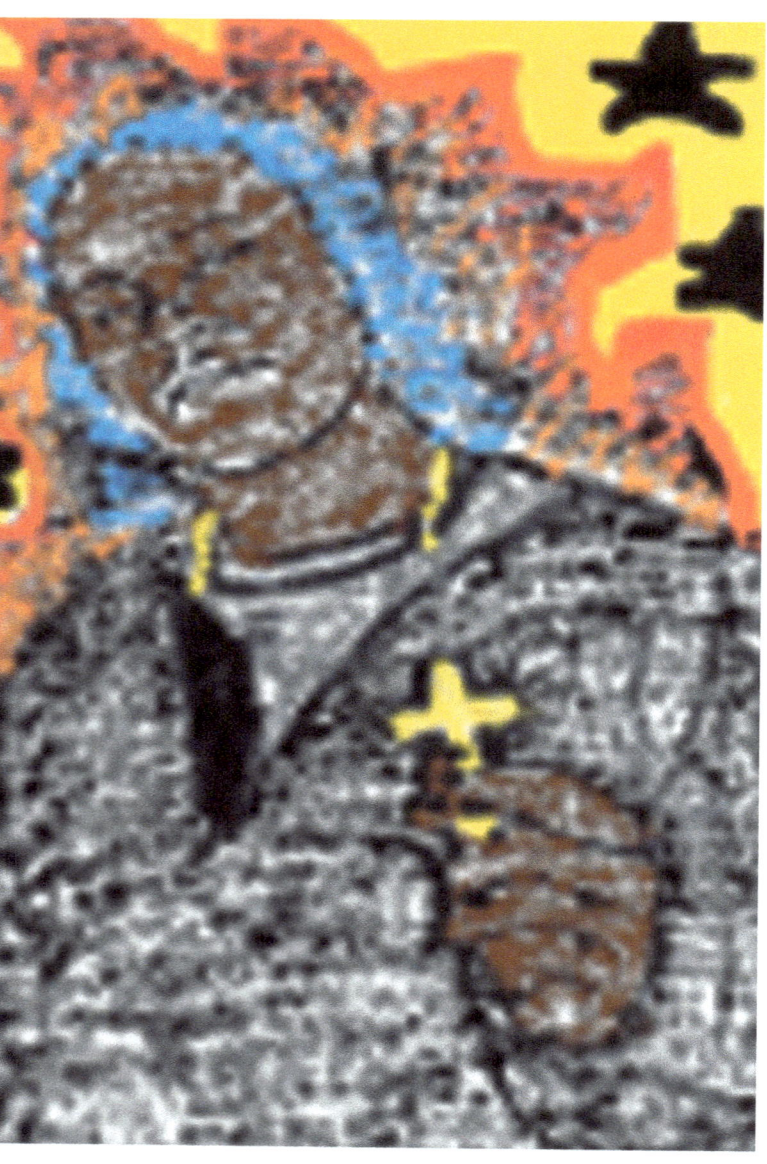

Headed for the stars
Reaching for the stars
Reaching every last heart desire
With a plan brewing in
the back of my mind
No sleeping this direction
Striving for perfection
Even when I'm tired
I'm on fire
No one can put out my flame
Headed for the stars
Overcoming anything
that comes my way
Beating the pain
Therefore beating the rain

By: Antony J. Gregory